Forgiveness

poems by

Chelsea Bunn

Finishing Line Press
Georgetown, Kentucky

Forgiveness

ACKNOWLEDGMENTS

Many thanks to the editors of the following publications where these poems
first appeared, sometimes in earlier versions:

Art in Odd Places: "Last Call"
Best New Poets 2018: "Litany"
Cover: "These Stories Are True"
Maudlin House: "Missed Connections"
ology: "Each Evening"
Sky Island Journal: "Saint Elizabeth"
Snapdragon: A Journal of Art & Healing: "Valentine's Day 2012: Last Message
From My Father"
Noble / Gas Qtrly: "The Beau Geste Effect"
The Big Windows Review: "Forgiveness"

Publisher: Leah Maines
Editor: Christen Kincaid
Cover Art and Design: Robert Christopher
Author Photo: Robert Christopher

Printed in the USA on acid-free paper.
Order online: www.finishinglinepress.com
also available on amazon.com

Author inquiries and mail orders:
Finishing Line Press
P. O. Box 1626
Georgetown, Kentucky 40324
U. S. A.

Table of Contents

"If you bring forth what is within you, what you bring forth will save you. If you do not bring forth what is within you, what you do not bring forth will destroy you."

— *The Gospel of Thomas*

Cancer

This is the year of awakening.
March promises you abundance.
December asks you to forgive.

Your thoughts will become clear:
smooth stones to pluck from a blue river.

Others look at you with reverence,
which at times becomes a burden.

It's hard for you to know
which voice to trust.

You're allowed to rest.
You're allowed stillness.

It can help to imagine anguish
as a small creature pawing at your hem,
wanting your attention.

The world will ask you
to humble yourself and fall into its arms.
It's a difficult task.

You know the temptation of withdrawal,
and you recognize darkness
when you hear its call,
like a train in the distance, like a dog
scratching at the door.

It is wise not to make your home
in the catacombs of worry.

Litany

Survived the father's   hand across
the kitchen table   that sudden sting
hand of passing   man/Canal Street
snaking   up my skirt
open hand of young   boy/crowded
corner/Mexico   twenty-three/older
man dragging leathered   hands across
my lifeless form   high school boy's
hands/my neck   I wouldn't let him
read my diary   city bus/man
across the aisle   busying his hand
in the unsound dark   his gaze a stain
a plague/a sore/a curse   but praise
the light that flickered   overhead
and banged us to a stop   somewhere
in Brooklyn   and praise
the door that delivered me   into
the night   and praise the body
its resilience   and praise the body
its resolve   and praise the body
its tender grief   and praise
the garbage disposal   of the mind
the neat waste it makes   of scraps

These Stories Are True

This poem is an erasure of the statements made by Senator Al Franken, Kevin Spacey, Harvey Weinstein, Jeffrey Tambor, and Louis C.K. (respectively) after they were accused of sexual misconduct.

1.

The first thing is the most
important thing.
Only you care—
I don't. I want something

good, hard,
shamefully obvious.

Picture millions of women
violated.

The intentions point to need.
Listen, I am the truth.

People deserve
to be let down.

2.

I have a lot.
I'm beyond.
I did owe him.
I carried him.
All these years.
Fueled by privacy.
Women have loved.
Men choose.
To live.
I want my own.

3.

I came
when I learned
anyone
needed
my absence.
All women
regret
hope.
Speak louder,
trust me.

I want,
and I plan.

I need
that anger.

My President,
perhaps I disappoint.

4.

huge
                    huge
            enormous
long
            often
predator
                    my flaws

5.

True,
I never learned
that power.

Asking
isn't a question.

These women—
I have
run from them.

I left
these women
cautious, disabled.

They tried,
I think,
to forgive,
which is nothing
to me,
a man given
to hurt.

And I can
hurt them all.

I love you,
my only
anguish:

people who have given me
anything I want.

The Beau Geste Effect

Up here there is no one
but me most days and
I've learned to quiet
myself when the coyotes
come yipping into the
crepuscular wind. *Beau
geste*, we've named the
distortion of their
scattered voices, their
auditory illusion: three
can sound like seven, two
like eight. Sometimes I
feel they are surrounding
me, fear they want to
drag me through dark
paths behind the houses
they circle.

Why did you leave your
life, they howl. Idiot. You
won't find a job, or
friends, and we watch the
smoke pour from your
chimney every night,
laughing at your
weakness. While you
sleep, we pace. We were
there the morning you
woke to fire in the west,
the morning you woke to
the peach tree split in
half, the morning you
woke to a dead owl in the
rain barrel. We knew
before you did. You will
never know how many
we are.

How You Found Me

In silence
   In black   & dis-
      avowed

Behind locked doors
scratching at my grave

Sleep-
less,
spine-
less,
      sunk

So drunk I couldn't stand
to eat a meal   or keep
my secrets from burning
me   to ash
Out back lighting cigarettes to still
my hands   from doing harm

To the blood moon, praying
   in an ancient   field

Ulcered, bright
      with shame &
   underdressed

A dog   tethered
     to a tree

Knee deep/in a river/casting
spells to make myself/a ghost

To Excess

I swallow flames.
I vibrate

like an atom, even
at absolute zero. I spin

like a leaf in a wind
tunnel. I deny myself

bread, meat, water.
I have no need.

My body knows
what to do to stay alive.

I soak up poison
until I erupt.

Do you think I care?
Watch me vomit

on a public bathroom floor.
Watch the rage

spill from my mouth
and watch me

turn away. I storm
across hemispheres

just to say *fuck you*. I
thunder I cyclone I

drought, gust,
monsoon. I disturb

your atmosphere,
a gravity wave born

by force. I keep
everything I feel.

I order my world
by sewing quilts

of blackened memories.
What is it

that I want?
Give me sweetness,

a steady hand
across my forehead.

Give me
what I deserve.

Give me
a dark room,

a decade,
a divorce.

I will bear it all and then
come back for more.

Last Call

I begged you not to let me go,
made you weep as if grieving
a loss on just your third day without me.

I sank myself inside
your memory, so that all
the men, all their faces,
the places you'd been, that long hour

in the evening, the prospect of being alone
drowned in me, blurred.
I wasted you. Ruined
dresses, whole mornings, a marriage,

almost. Left you
thoughtless, graceless.
Wrecked you. Had you
believe you'd never learn to leave.
Turned you sour, an angry bitch at thirty.

Pickled you wicked, fearful. Let you
cheat. Took your balance,
took your time & blotted it out.
A black hunger at the core
of you I filled.

I made you ache
for me. Whispered wishes on your lips,
rippled cool beneath your
fingertips. Made you dirty, got you lost.

Watched you drive with one eye shut
in broad daylight, weaving
down the road that led to me.

When it came time to pay,
you felt ashamed—flushed,
you flickered weak &

trembled, your every nerve lit
by plain, absolute longing.

The Meeting

The woman at the meeting told me
your disease will always be there
in your right ear telling you
to fuck it all up but in your left ear
is god telling you not to
and I thought oh great more voices
but let me back up
I was there
because my husband found
my fourth step inventory
and a fourth step inventory is where
you list whom you have harmed
and I had harmed him
but he didn't know
until he read it
on a crumpled piece of paper
in my awful handwriting
but let me back up again
I was there because
I couldn't stop drinking
and I couldn't stop drinking
because I am clinically depressed
and because that one voice always won
and because I didn't think I could live
any other way but to extinguish
every urge and pain and fear
before the light of day could expose
whatever truth I thought they held
and so I tried to tell the room
full of strangers what happened
but my voice kept cracking and
I felt my legs trembling in the metal chair
and I kept smashing my hands together
and then three women
surrounded me to stuff tissues in my palm
and give me their advice and I was surprised

because I'd only managed a few words really
and then the one—Sue—said the thing about the voices
and she said if he loves you
he will stay and he loves you doesn't he
and before this you're not guilty
and I loved her in that moment
I loved her gray eyes
and I loved her white t-shirt
and I loved her steady unwavering voice
and let me back up again
I was there because that is all I ever wanted—
for someone to see exactly
and entirely what I felt
and what I had done and to tell me
that it wasn't my fault
that I was sick but that I could get better
and for that to come not from pity
but from absolute understanding
and thank god for that woman
and god forgive me everything
and god direct my thinking
and god be the voice in my left ear
and please speak to me
loudly enough and soon enough
to save me from returning
to the dark room of my suffering

Procrastination

Because that last night I drove home from the hospital to nap,
    prolonging the decision I didn't know I'd have to make, trying to cast
    myself from the prospect of panic,

even though it was already in transit
    through my body—some sort of deep aortic
      work beyond the grasping of my traitor mind,
        which directed me to sleep—I missed his final gasps for air.

When the doctor called, I couldn't understand. I begged to move past
    jargon, until he finally, and quietly, delivered the most basic orders: No,
    you shouldn't wait. Yes. Come now.

When I returned, inexplicably intact,
    what must it have looked like? A portrait
    of raw nerves, a woman pant-
      ing like a stray dog as
        the doctor read his familiar transcript.

I couldn't take it. Wait, I said, and something buried was torn
    from me. I ran outside to vomit in a trash can.

We moved through the night like actors
    following a script.
      This is the daughter, wringing her hands. This is the son,
        stoic, tender. This is the coffee someone brought. Useless tonic.

And then that act
    was over. In the sunlit room, a pastor
      offered her services. Even that, I wouldn't accept. Not right now,
        I spit into the space between us, the imperceptible arc
          connecting my father to

me. Pure static,
        that space. There was nothing to do. There was no action
            left to take. Nowhere to get to. Was it a prison
                or was it freedom, the sudden absence of responsibility? My sin
                    had always been avoidance, my life a coin

I couldn't flip. But in that room, where one pain
        ended and another had begun, I clung to my husband, my brother,
            the pair of men who, it seemed, had made a silent pact

to hold me up in anticipation that
        because I waited to let my father love me, it
            would take me longer to come apart.

Inheritance

Days after our father has died, my brother and I are alone
in his apartment making piles of all he owned.
Here, the stamp collection he assured us
    one day be worth something. Here,

    the stained glass sun-catchers he'd hung
not in windows, but from the ceiling, dangling
down on fishing line to divide
    one room from the next.

In every pocket we find a toothpick, a crumpled tissue:
his earthly props. Always coughing, clearing
his throat, blowing his nose, utterly unashamed
    to make disgusting human noises.

A sorry stack of vintage Playboys
I let my brother deal with. I rifle through drawers, relentless,
wanting to clear out every dusty corner, empty every inch.
    I find a bundle of letters—

from the other daughter, old Air Force buddies,
one from his drunk daddy dictated
by his mother, who couldn't read or write.
    Those I save.

My brother wants it all. I want it gone.
I feel a fracture form between us, breaching the damp
basement air. We seem at odds. Determined, each, to choose for him
    what he never decided in life: what to keep, what to let go of.

We store the records. The good clothes
we donate, though I fear one day recognizing
his navy suit, his leather coat
    on another man.

  I fear we are pulling apart, that with each black bag
I drag to the curb, every discarded lamp or book or frame,
I am letting something slip away, letting him go,
    and I'm back in the hospital, before we know

    it is his last night, and I'm telling him
to stop complaining when he moans and I fear
I may never forgive myself for that,
    that final unkindness.

Forgiveness

Outside my therapist's office, three men are planting ferns,
  pruning bushes, cutting back the tangled vines
    that twine across the building's bricks, covering them in green,

and when I reach the door one of them has risen,
  nods his head, and it seems a nod that verges
    on pity, as if he's seeing

into the room I'll enter to empty myself of grief
  and wants to offer
    one gesture before turning back to the roses,

a projection I should share
  but never will. Inside, I settle
    in the chair across from her, the woman

I see each week despite my fear of being seen.
  Have you thought over,
    she asks, what we talked about last time? She's trying

to get me to forgive
  myself. She wants to free me
    of the song

I play over and over
  in my mind, which governs
    every part of me: nerves,

veins,
  fingers,
    ego.

I sing
  myself my sins:
    Clear, dry gin.

The man I loved (my roving
   heart). The fringes
      that I occupied. My father

in his hospital bed and I
   too late. What severing
      it must take to let this go.

And now she says, moving a little closer to the edge
   of her chair, really seeing
      me, or

wanting to, I had a patient once,
   in a place far from here, who,
      in the impenetrable fog

of her disorders, and guided by some sick version
   of herself, killed her three little sons.
      And when she came

to see me, after the fever
   of her sin
      had burned the memory to fine

dust, she didn't even
   know what she had done.
      And I had to decide—do I

tell her what she did? And now an ambulance goes
   by outside. I follow the noise
      of its thin siren

dragging itself down the street until it's gone,
   and those men, I suppose, are finishing
      their work, satisfied by having given

life to that garden, and the garden, content
   in being tended to, everything green
      and free

to bloom. She says:
I didn't tell her.

Valentine's Day 2012:
Last Message from My Father

Hi honey

      I just, uh,
            it's, uh, quarter to one
       and I just called to see if you would

please

be my Valentine, um,

alright alright alright
I know
I'm kidding
but anyway I do love you
and I wish you have a I hope you have a
           happy   day

      and go to lunch with your husband
           and this and
           and this and that and
      give your puppies a hug for me—

call me sometime
tonight if you want to honey
I love you very much
        you're a very special girl

okay bye bye

Reunion

They're at that French café again, where they always
used to meet. He holds the door, saying please,
his arm a long curve of invitation.

She remembers what her ex told her—that when men do this
they are trying to look at your ass. He chooses
a table. She fingers the sugar packets in their little plastic box.

He's back from Austin, showing her
pictures of the sonogram on his phone. He's telling her
too many details about the girl
switching birth control, she pictures him

above her, feels a sharp urge
to reach over and just
touch his arm, just a little.

He asks about her father's death. She's abbreviating, giving
just the highlights, skipping ahead, repeating.
She hasn't taught herself the story yet.

Sorry, he's saying. *I'm so sorry.* She stirs
and stirs the straw in her glass,
knocking the ice around, her whole body
humming with heat and grief,

overcome with unmet need, suddenly convinced
that everything, everyone—the waitresses in their black shirts,
the exquisite ringing after two wine glasses have clinked together—

is crashing against her,
and the word *relief* keeps coming
to her, banging through her brain,
a wild bird thrashing its wings,

and what should she do in this moment,
unable to see him again, unable
to ever tell him she's sorry, she's so sorry?

Missed Connections

Waiting for the downtown 6 at 5 o'clock,
my other life comes rushing back in waves.

A man straps an accordion to his chest, opens
and closes its bellows, delivering long columns

of sound into the stagnant August air.
Across the platform, pairs of schoolchildren

march in procession, arms linked as if when someone
knows who you are, you won't get left behind.

You: two years absent, phantom that I drag around.
Me: one year sober, still locked inside myself.

Still sequestered, still on edge.
Private in my infuriating grief—

waking daily from the dream of my father in his hospital bed,
ventilator squeezing and sucking at his chest even after he is gone,

after the blonde nurse has wrapped her clean arms around me,
after the long, low moan of the monitor.

The early morning light blasting through the windows.
The things I couldn't say.

Petition

Lord, hear my prayer and give me clean
thoughts. Give me anything to lean
against, please, or deliver air
that sweeps my face and shoulders bare
and lets me still the loud machine

that rattles in my head unseen.
Give me clarity, the citrine
light of sunrise. Not anywhere,
Lord. Here. My prayer

goes howling through the evergreens,
my prayer, bright as a tangerine
and as sweet, for you, if you're there,
or here, oh, Lord, give me, I swear,
Lord, hear my prayer.

Each Evening

she walks the backyard
plucking heads off flowers.
Her father is teaching her

to garden: this is what keeps them
alive—removing atrocities, brittle
iterations of loss.

Something in this angers her—
the hardened petals
of each flower

dying differently,
and she has no choice
but to crumble

between her fingers
their red and orange ruin.
Marigolds, the golden disasters,

stuck like sculptures
to their stems.
Petunias, the blooms

impetuous knives,
easily detached. She dreads
this complicity

each evening—separating the dead
from the living, pulling scorched
blades from their graves,

as if she is somehow
to blame, as if with her
devastation, summer ends.

Saint Elizabeth

When we speak her name, we are
so quiet, the air around us distilled.

He says, *It's worse at night,* and I know
that means he wakes up, she's gone

from the bed they shared for decades,
and he can't stop sobbing. We are

standing in their kitchen, every-
thing of hers still in its place, even

her cell phone silent on the counter.
What color is this? he asks, and reaches

for my hair. I don't move, my back
to him, my body tense in its own sorrow,

and I feel his fingers drift over the tangles
hanging down my shoulders. For a moment

I am in some other place, in danger—
of what, I couldn't say—but I try

his grief therapist's exercise, repeating
to myself *I am here, I am in my body, I am*

breathing, and then
I understand that all this is

is just one man
missing one woman, a loss

in which I play an incidental role.
It's not mine, none of this is,

really, and he says, *I'm sorry—*
I miss certain things and I say,

I know, although I don't, and he's moved
away from me now, rifling through a cabinet

for tea, crossing the room to open
a window. It's spring: a far cry

from the bitter January morning
when we buried her. The singular fact,

both a shock and a comfort,
that time moves on, that so much

time has moved on, and still so little, rarefies
the air sweeping in to touch our living skin.

Desert Impasse

Blonde grasses
dry clean and brittle
in January's winds.

Two thousand miles away
my father died.

What I'd hoped
may not be true:

that here, all grief
collapses like a star,
its matter ejected into space.

That here, all sins
are turned to dust.

Chelsea Bunn is a poet and educator living in New Mexico. Her work appears in publications in print and online, including *Best New Poets 2018, Sky Island Journal, Maudlin House, Apathy Magazine, The Ellis Review, Cover, The Big Windows Review, Big City Lit*, and other journals and anthologies.

She earned her MFA in Poetry and her BA in English at Hunter College in New York, where she received a teaching fellowship, a Norma Lubetsky Friedman Scholarship, and taught creative writing for eleven years. She was selected as Thinker in Residence by Art in Odd Places in 2016, was a finalist for the Lit Fest Fellowship for Emerging Writers in 2018, was awarded the Academy of American Poets Prize twice, and was named a Best New Poet of 2018. Her poems have received recognition from The National Federation of State Poetry Societies, Poetry Society of America, Lighthouse Writers Workshop, Georgetown Review, and elsewhere.

Born and raised in NYC, she currently serves as Assistant Professor of Creative Writing for the Bachelor of Fine Arts program at Navajo Technical University.

CPSIA information can be obtained
at www.ICGtesting.com
Printed in the USA
LVHW030124060919
630110LV00001B/39